THE COMPANY OF CHILDREN

THE COMPANY OF CHILDREN

Poems by Barry Spacks

DOUBLEDAY & COMPANY, INC.

GARDEN CITY, NEW YORK

The poems, FRESHMAN; LONG SONG, A WIFE SONG, A CAT SONG, A RAIN SONG; THE OUTRAGEOUSLY BLESSED appeared originally in *The New Yorker*. The poem FINGERS appeared originally in *The Massachusetts Review* as A STUDY OF FINGERS, Copyright © 1963 The Massachusetts Review, Inc., and is reprinted with permission. Also, the poems THE SOLITARY AT SEVENTEEN, ROBERT'S SONG, REC-OMMENDATIONS and OCTOBER appeared originally in *Poetry*, Copy-right © 1960, 1966, 1967 by Modern Poetry Association. Other poems appeared in *The Carleton Miscellany, Shenandoah, Folio, Keynote, Quince, Can, Audit, The Chicago Review, The Yale Review, The Beloit Poetry Journal, The Nation, The Critical Quarterly, Mademoiselle, The American Scholar, The Little Square Review*. The poem THE WORLD AS A VISION OF THE UNITY IN FLESH appeared in *Noble Savage* No 2, Copyright © 1960 The World Publishing Company, and the poem MY CLOTHES appeared in *The Sewanee Review*, Copyright © 1967 by The University of the South.

Library of Congress Catalog Card Number 68–14176

Copyright © 1958, 1960, 1961, 1962, 1963, 1964, 1965, 1966, 1967, 1968, 1969 by Barry Spacks

All Rights Reserved

Printed in the United States of America

First Edition

For my wife and my daughter

CONTENTS

THE COMPANY OF CHILDREN

I

BLIND IN HIS SORROW

Blind in his sorrow and his fitful joy
he travels through the tangled wood of self
while she moves on beside him, meadow-sweet.

He blunders in the dark, afraid to see
how always she, beside him and before
makes everywhere a clearing; everywhere.

He stands upon his shadow's shrunken noon,
and if he'd take one step he'd come into
her love, that waits for him, a summer field.

FRESHMEN

My freshmen
settle in. Achilles
sulks; Pascal consults
his watch; and true
Cordelia—with her just-washed hair,

stern-hearted princess, ready to defend
the meticulous garden of truths in her highschool notebook—
uncaps her ballpoint pen.
And the corridors drum:
give us a flourish, fluorescence of light, for the teachers come,

green and seasoned, bearers
of the Word, who differ
like its letters; there are some
so wise their eyes
are birdbites; one,

a mad, grinning gent with a golden tooth, God knows
he might be Pan, or the sub-
custodian; another
is a walking podium, dense
with his mystery—high

priests and attachés
of the ministry; kindly
old women, like unfashionable watering places;
and the assuming young, rolled tight as a City
umbrella;

thought-salesmen with samples cases,
and saints upon whom
merely to gaze is like Sunday—
their rapt, bright,
cat-licked faces!

And the freshmen wait;
wait bristling, acned, glowing like a brand,
or easy, chatting, munching, muscles lax,
each in his chosen corner, and in each
a chosen corner.

Full of certainties and reasons,
or uncertainties and reasons,
full of reasons as a conch contains the sea,
they wait: for the term's first bell;
for another mismatched wrestle through the year;

for a teacher who's religious in his art,
a wizard of a sort, to call the roll
and from mere names
cause people
to appear.

The best look like the swinging door
to the Opera just before
the Marx Brothers break through.
The worst—debased,
on the back row,

as far as one can go
from speech—
are walls where childish scribbling's been erased;
are stones
to teach.

And I am paid to ask them questions:
Dare man proceed by need alone?
Did Esau like
his pottage?
Is any heart in order after Belsen?

And when one stops to think, I'll catch his heel,
put scissors to him, excavate his chest!
Watch, freshmen, for my words about the past
can make you turn your back. I wait to throw,
most foul, most foul, the future in your face.

WASHING WINDOWS

for Laura and Herb Jackson

On a ladder, in an old checkered shirt,
he takes the rag she offers from within.
Their hands begin
slowly to circle, polishing,
and for a time, as particles
on a field of force align,
their hands move one to one,
tight, in a dance, and the glass goes bright
between them, hard, a clearing lens.
They pause and smile, at peace,
each in his own condition.

IN THE CALM AND MEASURED COUNTRY

In the calm and measured country of my sleep, last night
I woke, woke without motion,
and without motion in the dark so dark that I knew nothing
there was no end of me,
I was as shapeless as the moment of my waking.

I heard my father, heard him thrusting, working
upon his deathbed's wrinkled country,
and measureless with fear I lay beside you.
My father's love and then his stillness
rolled through to be the night I roamed in,

as if through water where I heard
a fumble: rustle: heard a someone something
at the latch.
It was our daughter turning.
It was our daughter, turning in her sleep.

THE PHILOSOPHER AND HIS WIFE

"Confusion is the seed of grace."
I say this to her tidy face.
I breathe it in her formal ear.
The uncut grass in the rain I hear.

Her ease is blasphemy of pain.
She smiles away the wind and rain.
She smiles; at once the weather's gone;
we pace the comfort of the lawn.

"The nine disguising heavens hide
God's dancing form; unmystified,
you mime His movements, clear and strict.
Such is the anguish you inflict."

The weather's wind in sudden surge
makes mist of speech. I pray a scourge
of rain to whip her calmness down;
to spot her tasteful silken gown.

"There's more to ease than meets the eye,"
she says. Above her head the sky
arranges clouds to suit her dress;
and who will fathom my distress?

THE WORLD AS A VISION OF THE UNITY IN FLESH

Every Paris in the morning
when the mist is on the street
all the lovers fall to dreaming
nose to nose and feet to feet,
through the small-talk of the dawning
like one body in their heat.

While the faithful dogs are yawning,
while the suicides are scheming,
all the lovers fall to dreaming
in this clearinghouse of woes;
all the lovers fall to dreaming
and their dreams are bittersweet;

all the lovers fall to dreaming
and they dream their dreams of those
lying under clumsy covers
close beside their newer lovers,
who are dreaming dreams of others,
feet to feet, and nose to nose.

FATHER FIGURE

1

You are a figure like the sun,
all witness, all one eye.
Your daily shrug can fan the children
wild, or leave them frozen,
or blind them with a vision
of power.
You send an invitation
with no address
to a dance—
and they could weep, the children,
they could feed on clay—
you neither ask them is it thus and so
nor keep them from themselves, your will
their punctuation.

2

Come close upon them.
Why give them room, full chance to shine,
when they feel better, less themselves,
lost in your glow?
It is your distance makes them throw
each other down the drain;
your justice makes them dream
of a stormtrooper, of the pleasure
of the drill.
How they wish to despise you, you and your freedom!
You neither go, nor help them,
and they are licking blood, are leaping from the housetops,
that you might catch them, or whip them,
or show them how to fly.

BIRD AND WORM

A grackle snaps a worm from my balding lawn;
half a worm, anyway: handout from grudging nature.
Then, bird, why don't you chew? He cocks his head;
he's set up like a car lot hero
with an early morning sale.
He's getting fatter on sheer *gloire*.
He thinks: By God, God loves me!

And the piece of worm, string-
tatter in a catchy wind,
flaps grass, tossed up
some inches, and down comes less,
less length, more wiggle,
as grackle pecks and poses,
aiming blind.

He'll get it all; it's money in the bank.
I dig this bird's
sufficiency: *his* eye is on patrol.
Nervous; nervous;
he's somebody else's mouthful.
He breakfasts like a long talk with a cop.
Like a lover with a quick ear for the latch.

I think I'll stop
at this. Grab, grackle; snatch
by instruments:
the quicker half
of that worm is going
very fast
deep down.

THE TRUE APOSTLE

The true apostle
to the sanctimonious
makes a bad bedfellow.
How he'll toss and turn!

Always ten faster, unsavory guys
get in there with the beeping message first,
crying Lord, Lord, in neon,
in firecrackers, with dancing girls.

And about the careful true one
there grow up factions:
Hassidic Platonists
unmasked as Manichees,

would-be chiropodists,
cuticle-clippers who couldn't be less
taken with wine:
all after bread.

But entrepreneurs he can handle; they run
from the wolf.
His problem is how to be leapy
and not cause backlash.

A home waits all comfy for him
among the Pharisees;
and the gentiles are restless,
and have their flashy leaders.

Will he blend deftly
into the scenery?
Or steer a middle course, or wear a rhinestone sandwichboard?
Will he beg, or steal, or borrow?

Tune in tomorrow.

EXERCISES

1 *The Rose*

Take a rose, a nominal rose,
in the mind's hand.
Do not lip it, or smell it,
but as the waves of a new thought rise
throw it, your rose,
and see it glide.
Now attempt
to prevent
its return
on the tide.

2 *The Onion*

A large, lusty one.
Strip it, make it young again,
and with the tip of the tongue,
or the pale inside of the arm,
or with the nose or the chin
deal with its smoothness, its curving
skin within skin.

Now cut it,
though you weep,
and fit it
back together.
Have you lost
the wrapper?
Will the wound knit? will it heal?
There is no need
to repeat this exercise.

3 The Egg

Having embraced yourself
in the fetal position,
you are the yellow,
the air is the white,
the house is the shell.

What cracks the house?
What strains the air
to get at you?
It is the world.
Peck its hand!

LONG SONG, A WIFE SONG,
A CAT SONG, A RAIN SONG

Our cat is climbing for a jay
in the apple tree. The lawn is brown.
These jays are clearly anti-cat.
He mounts the tree, they shout him down;

from banderillas of the beak
he slinks away, so whipped he'd vote
for dogs; he kicks a modest bug;
and slowly as a hangman's rope

we swing. Oh, wife, we're suburbed, bagged,
and you must hear the mouth you wed
insisting nothing comes to much
but dust. That sentence is unsaid

when soon as silk you grace my touch.
Then rain becomes a state of mind
and every leaf expects a kiss,
and every knot is cut, or kind.

But only irrepairs increase.
The urgencies of loving end.
We once knew days like honing wind;
it snowed: God stroked the living fleece;

it rained: God saved the saving rain
that fell as hard as seagulls' eyes.
We're mourning down to dustbin size,
and all the local lawns make hay,

and in this hammock someone sleeps
who must be me—he dreams like me—
a dream of birth: to leave the bag
the sagging parts are jumbled in.

A knitting of intents goes on,
sleep's patchwork, healings of the cave.
Remade, triumphal up the nave
in childly joy, in drenching robes,

I wake to dry beneath the sun.
My sleep has washed me with its paws
in dreams of rain when I was young.
I'm back where jays scream zoning laws.

Where *was* I? Dreaming what I was.
Oh, vintage wits and cleanly claws,
the tide's gone out and won't come in;
what gives, if something else much more's

to follow? Cupped in empty hands,
the air says "*Wind* is what I mean."
The earth says "Harvest is my say."
The cat stands by, and understands.

ι, wife, come sing a hopeful song!
cat will reach a likely limb.
's dusty, rain come loud and long.
kinky, sleep unravel him.

v the taproot find a spring,
ιry plant ride up its stalk's
ike! Start the countdown, love—
he roof of the greenhouse off

rain. God save the rain.
ot and branch of me.
eeping. Love me, love.
ιp the apple tree.

THE COMPANY OF CHILDREN

for James Baker Hall

Desire may soar
from the valleys weightlessly
as in those nature films at school
where insects swell to premature old age
or sudden trees
surge up from seed to fruit
burning with power.

But the world, at its own good speed,
is tugged by oxen.

A house will not rise at a word;
its rafters will not lie
patient in mid-air,
but must be muscled there;
struck humble.

The builder drives
his sharp ax in the wood,
across the natural fall
of speech and light.

To raise a house he leaves
dream-flight, and all thought of ease,
of instant mastery
of talents, instruments:
the hope that leaps
for a glimpse of the Garden.

And leaves the company of children;
of those who'd prove by crashing into trees
that forests are against them;
of those who'd have the Muse
—unwooed, ripe, incoherent girl—
fall in their laps with the smell
of bitten apples.

A house is raised
as one would go to mount a hill,
growing smaller as the hill
grows taller as he nears, until,
upon it,
fixed foot and quest foot, the hill
disappears; becomes
a topless tower; becomes
forever.

When at the top he stands, well pleased,
stands high with himself, he stands amazed:
the hill is smaller,
for he is taller
by a hill.

He builds his house,
and then returns
to the company
of children.

THREE SONGS FOR MY DAUGHTER

1

Simply as the world is turning
toward the ashes and the fuel,
toward the secret of the burning
simply as the world is turning
children cross the road to school.

Many come to less by growing
once the autumn's courses start.
Daughter, in the place you're going
many come to less by growing,
losing what they've had by heart.

Simply as the world is turning,
scholar hand in hand with fool,
to a learning and unlearning
simply as the world is turning
children cross the road to school.

2

Child, where we stand
is quicksand.

This venerable crust
dust.

Move bravely on,
as if there were watchers.

3

Daughter, you will reach a twilight
clear as joy: a summer evening
when the small bells ring and fingers
stir within too swift for meaning.
Take the hand of your beloved;
in the bell of stillness gathered
time will seem to pause for you.
Dear passenger: just so, so still
with us, until the rhyme for darkness
booms—booms as if the feathers
of all scattered birds were falling.
Night comes. Our voices, pounding,
are the bells
that will your love.

II

SINCERITY: A DEFINITION

for P.M.S.

"Your bait of falsehood takes this carp
of truth" HAMLET, II,i

Not on the one hand *whimsy*,
  heliumed out of sight,
    nor on the other *cliché*,
      which some call "observation,"

but quite simply,
  from my own, home-grown O.E.D.,
    discovery; i.e.,
      telling lies

that tempt the fish of Truth to rise
  striking from mud-bottom into light,
    open-mouthed for flies
      made out of feathers.

JURY DUTY

Summoned, I feel like Joseph K.
The panel gathers on this day after May Day.
The court clerk in flannels sucks a mint
matching the cold, hospital scent.
Striped silk, the flag by the judgment seat
sags like a flogging. My eyes meet
wood panels, finial fleurs-de-lis:
a termite's Miami. Behind me these
forty-some peers; the mothers, exempted,
stay on to judge the back of my head,
self-trimmed and ragged. Who's after blood?
Forbidden to read or write, I chew cud,
look toward the ceiling where golden scales
depend from starlight, a setting sun pales,
and the balance is struck on the haft of a sword.
The panel rustles, heavily bored.
Elsewhere an oxbow holds weighing pans;
or a cross. All's empty. Chatter begins.
The microphone's mute, the slide-screen encased,
the exhibit table undefaced
by weapons; the blackboard actually white;
and down through the milk-glass roof falls sunlight
dead neutral. At either end of the bar,
switched on, bronze and orange, are
Tiffany lamps. We owe to whom—
to the State?—this touch of the living room?
To the Judge. He's late. We stiffly sit
and wait. We hate the Judge a bit,
which puts us in a human mood.
We wait until our pores exude
our waiting. Neighbors start to nudge
and whisper. Someone goes to cadge
a cigarette; another does
his paper up and offers it
around. We're reaching common ground,
and the clerk's off combing out the curls
of the Judge and all his dancing girls.

THE WANDERING JEW AT THE UENO PARK ZOO

Within their park the high giraffes
make nibbling love amid the trees.
The children throw them peanuts but
they bow to me on knobby knees.

The otter swims his pool, my heart;
the weasel furrows in my blood;
and lurching to embrace me comes
the bear whose breast is warm as God.

I watch the peacock spread his fan:
the parents hold their infants high to see
his quivering bush of a thousand eyes;
his real eye riveted on me.

HOMAGE TO HENRY JAMES

The drum roll swells, and a hesitant foot
tiptoes the wire—he runs, he leans,
a spectator groans, "Oh dear, he'll fall!"
But he *holds*, he's *firm*, and a golden ball
that's been knocking about in his Norfolk jacket
engrossing itself in the easterly pocket
for many long years, looms lucently up,
lofts languidly up and up. *Applause.*
It's just a balloon of a ball of a small
sort of side-wheeling clause, with no purpose or cause
so it seems, and he mugs, and he putters and dreams
while his feet mince the more-or-less
perilous wiry ways;
as he shifts, as he squints, as he pauses
he *sways*
and the young people squeal, but no more of that:
another gold ball squeezes out of his hat!
Then more, and more: they roll, they rest,
the seventh steps over the third at last
and James slipshods with a Chaplin stance—
his umbrella is open, he's doing a dance
(applause, applause!)—he gravely nods
to a passing ball, and frowns at another:
they glintingly, glaringly circle each other,
bounce and cascade from his juggling hands
as he swiftly proceeds on his humorous hams
and reaches the platform unruffled of hair—
with, as who should say, all his balls in the air.

THE OUTRAGEOUSLY BLESSED

The gods would have us chastened through confusion,
so those who tempt the skies' outrage are blessed.
Though Zeus might be a cupboy for the thanks he gets
from these,
the pretty boys who'd fall asleep
disputing with slow Socrates,
they're still the ones who catch the key equations
and laugh to straw the schoolmen and the schools;
they win the game by changing all the rules.

Small comfort to the sane, who do their best,
to find we cherish maddening exceptions:
the lines that need not scan; the gulfs in nature;
the odds and irritants our cosmic oyster
cannot digest
as the pearl grows precious in its queer success.

FINGERS

Swift, like stunted snakes entrapped
in wider, sluggish mothers, fingers
arch to bite their buried tails.

Trained to be retrievers, grasping,
sullen of the nether lip;
or wild as dancing children, or, like rhinos,

dangerous at the tip
and carapaced and lined: designed
like hairy cushioned roots, these creepers,

sometime lovers, makers, leapers,
clenched, are staring moonfaced watchers;
village elders, blind as twigs.

AN OBSERVATION OF THE HUSBAND
IN THE MARKET PLACE

He'd say his history concerned
himself and wife and child alone.
He spins like a fiery mote. He burns,
a mote of sun within the sun.

A purely local hero, father,
earnest seeker, twin-bed lover,
gyroscopic blur, he'd bother
any buyer, his receiver

never on the hook; he dials
and swivels daily to the fray.
He's stirring all his wits and wiles
together; love must light his way,

for every feather in his cap
has gone to line the nest of home;
poor dog, he never steals a nap
but falls to dreaming of a bone.

His milder, courtly forebears took
more leisure, even in the game
where lies no knight could overlook
were challenged; where no man was tame.

But he, dear God, the things he'll do,
the jousts, the deeds; the cause, the cause!
Each day he runs Medusa through,
and whittles baubles from her claws.

BIRTHDAY

Don't mention the rocks, the blocks from the quarries, the
  boulders . . .
I've work that is heavy enough in the dust of the gravel.
Far off in the distance they heave a few Alps on their
  shoulders.
I shudder, and bend my back low, and search with my
  tweezers.

More wise than my child when a wave leaps the moat of her
  castle,
I clear a new space, I sift through the thousands of pieces.
In shade from my arching body my fingers rustle,
and out where it's simple they lever the slab of Australia.

I laid out some stones, half-inches that looked like each other,
and rose, and stumbled, and scattered the ends of my labor.
How did it fit? how did it all fit together?
Behind me the children are digging a hole to China.

MY CLOTHES

Poor spineless things, the clothes I've shed
in hopes of the essential bed
of love. Like chastened dogs they wait
to be forgiven, stroked, pulled straight.
I lift them to the light, all holes
and patches, all the outworn roles,
the Dandy's musty ornaments,
the Lover's, and the Malcontent's.
The day seeks like a wind its form;
my clothes have kept me from the storm.
From age to age though I emerge
from cloying silks or common serge
my mere limbs stutter in the sun;
outside the cave, I come undone.
O, voices in your nakedness,
great dreamers in your skins or less,
make golden ages fill my mind
where ease leaves agony behind
and passion, all her raiment gone,
is beautiful with nothing on.

DAY FULL OF GULLS

Slow as the tide, a lifeguard smooths
his gritty girl, and seagulls stand
and the shadows of clouds appear like pools
and the waves fall back on themselves like sleep.

Day full of gulls, a storm of gulls,
wheel within wheel of caw and sweep,
never seeing enough of them,
how they tilt the air, and glide, and ebb.

At noon in the surf some raucous boys
made them scream like themselves, wings batting bodies,
vicious for lumps of last week's bread.
Day full of gulls. A storm of gulls.

Now women cast out evening crusts
like a sowing of love, and fathers aim
bits plucked like cake crumbs from the loaf,
to be snapped in mid-air with stern elegance.

A girl in the drift of the sea edge leans
on tiptoe, skirts held up. A gull
ends flight, like an indrawn breath,
on the small of his shadow.

THE MUSE

The Muse came pulling off her gown
and nine feet tall she laid her down
and I by her side a popinjay
with nothing to say. Did she mean to stay?

She smelled like flame, like starch on sweat,
like sperm; like shame; like a launderette.
No one, she said, *has loved me right.*
Day and night. Day and night.

III

A LETTER

Where you are, a fly on a pool of pitch or honey
buzzes and waits, considers, strikes out and stumbles.
Or a horse with his cart: if he stops, he stands in the traces,
and if he went burdenless still he would know in his haunches
the strain, the familiar strain, and for that be thankful.

I know where you are; and yet I would have you be
elsewhere: reclining at morning on a veranda
above the sea, drowsy, still in your nightdress,
your face to the sun, to the breakers, the smell of the coffee;
a brilliant white bowl with peaches and melon beside you.

I think of Houdini, lowered by pride in the harbor
sealed in a coffin, limbs fettered, around him dark water;
and strong in his skill he mounts, his broken chains trailing;
the shackles assume a new shape in his furious fingers.
Old artist—Houdini—brave swimmer: how is it going?

THE SOLITARY AT SEVENTEEN

Made double by his lust
he sounds a woman's groans.
A figment of his flesh
she swoons: the final thrust
has rattled both their bones.
Now in his organs where
she lies tupped half to death,
drinking his body's air,
wheezing behind his breath,
she, without warmth or shame,
whispers her separate name.

THE CHANGING

Your kiss has made my mouth as smooth as light.
Made it your mouth, my face your face I wear,
your body on me that I can't wipe off;
like the glow of a daffodil
it echoes from my skin.

I am no deeply brighter now,
no stronger than I've ever been.
This newness on my lips can't heal your eyes.
And yet you gaze; you touch me like Miranda;
you touch me, and we shine.

Oh, but our bodies take such sweetness on!
Meeting, they barter, children jealous of the other's gift.
Changing, our bodies are like children,
blind children in their mother's house,
who know their way.

DANDY

Everybody has a few certain chords
and it pleases them to make those noises.
As the poet's fey wife says, reading an ad
for a thigh-high green voile dress: "I
buy my own size, which is for myself,
and I try it: for yummy, for *baby*
here I am. This fetches me, so
live a little, raise the hem, like
how many legs have you got?"

Meanwhile, asweat, the poet
spears dandelions, with a new device, a rigidified
snake's tongue. He's keeping up
with Neighbor in his Swiss Chalet
who clips the lawn three times a day.
And in the lawn, dandelions are so *hope*ful
if you cut a head off it turns to seed.
As soon as poet zoncks one out, another
sits down behind him.

At the rate he's digging eventually
the lawn, the house, the trees, the fence will go;
he'll be hopping on the hot iron core,
wrestling the final root.
"Hey," I greet him, "Djerkopf! why not pull
the grass, which is meeker? You'll never get anywhere
with these egomaniacs." But he:
"I live in this country, and by God
I'll make the right impression."

He climbs from the ditch where the world used to be;
mounts high up his mound of dopy weeds, and sits;
takes from them all a dandy,
and says its leaves
are like child-drawn Christmas trees, and of its head:
"That's how *Gorgons* look in a sunny clime."
He finds his key. "These," he hums, "are interfered with, yet
  say
their own size, and for their own selves
persist."

And takes out paper, a pen, a lens, to keep
account; to give
meticulous attention: i.e., love.
Wilting in the sun, and awed, he scans
like a U2 a moony
globe; a family
of budniks; a *bon vivant*, asprawl, at ease in dirt;
and a tall, tense one, all its candles
lit.

TO THE PHOTOGRAPHER OF A THORN TREE

These thorns were not forged metal till you got there,
ordering light
to hold in its passing
so even the shadows
of thorns would seem to heal.

They were of thornflesh, mutable;
of fiber, that rots.
They were and are of fiber, that ice will case-in hard;
that men intent on flattened ground
uproot.

They were and are
forming always out of sap,
forming to a point, a jut of pain;
thrusting in the heated season;
proud of their want.

Here, you have calmed them to a scheme.
They rest in their transcendence;
they cannot alter.
And you go on, to tulips and to weeds:
through with them.

FISHING ON A SNOWY RIVER
(after a painting attributed to Hsü Tao-ning)

for Caren Dallett

An ox on the roadway the size of a bread crumb;
a bridge and a bush; a hut and a boulder;
the springtide descending; the wind in the treetops;
the mountains, mountains, curved for joy.

And one knuckle high, a fisherman fishing;
motionless, down by the snowy river.
Above him the mountains recede, are silk;
his line meets the water, and that is all.

A bridge and a bush, a hut and a boulder,
and mountains, mountains, treacherous forms
swept over and over, the shape of speed.
It's spring in the mountains, and in those mountains

where is the fisherman? where will I find him?
Stately he stands in the silent valley.
Half an inch high, he is motionless, fishing.
Above him the mountains recede; are silk.

His line meets the water.

ON THE DEATH OF GIACOMETTI

He whose despair
became a way of speech
lies now beyond all care
or reach.
He lived for nothing but his work:
to raise his shadow from the dark.

Struck once in traffic, Sartre claims, he said
"At last, something has happened!"
He sculpted
disasters; he captained
ship by welcoming
the waves aboard, and with a crazing

joy drove on his crew
by flailing with his hammer at the ones
unworthy to be reverenced into
bronze.
It was of artistry he died:
the failure, ever, to be satisfied.

Now his own substance is destroyed,
who knew no certitude
but set thin lengths against the void,
thin roots of plenitude.
Now earth, that labors toward precision,
begins his long, last revision.

AN EMBLEM OF TWO FOXES

Simply to breathe
can make him bleed,
the fox whose leg
is trapped, whose will
awaits the kill.
Why should he flail?
Moving hurts,
so he lies still.

Around him walks
a prouder fox,
his severed leg
a homily
on going free,
as if to say
it hurts, it hurts
either way.

ROBERT'S SONG

for Robert David Cohen

The light survives
the fading of its voice;
quasars quaver: where am I
taking place?
How shall I join the confines of attention,
that I may quote
from the long dispatch
and when the focus blurs, tune the instruments
by love?
O partner, take my senses like a glove;
o move upon me like a wind of light

    move like a wind to shoulder the trance of my silence
    into the world again; into
    the world.

For lonely the spirit broods in its little room,
blinded by preening feathers, thundered
dumb;
from the ingrown eye gaining hatred
of the head;
gaining hatred, till the very universe
grows weary; tires
of the journey; falls
back upon itself, down the hole of itself;
its
singularity.

    Though I stir like a lifting of leaves before the storm:
    though the brightness leaps in the light like a breath
        intaken:
    I shall fall, and soak up my shadow like a sponge.

There is no other I may call in my extremity;
no man may tell me
I of my exile earn
free passage;
that I am worthy, worthy,
that I may leave the provinces
of Doubt;
that by peculiar
pausings of the breath I shall become
a singular quiddity, lasting beyond
the skin.

In the land of good counsel, I am the capital city.
I choose my speed: I am my only hitchhiker.
On fields of rare wishes, I am the wind and sun.

And so to chance. How can I do irrelevance? My feet
are summer squash, on the long vines of my blood.
I am the bride on her mule; the salt of my salting;
I am the spangled girl in the sawdust pit;
I sing to my soul not to mourn for the dust upon it;
I choose my speed, I praise the stores of my body,
worms that would spice my soil: tides of the lung!
Drums of the ear, o chests of the little tools!
Be welcome, buttocks that bring me the news of the chair!
Be welcome, handsful of fingers that mean to bless!
Pronounce the quiddity: prepare me my elephant:

I go
to cast
a shade.

IV

AT 35

Father, what would you make of me? I wear your face.
I hear my cough and think the worms have sent you home.
Here at my table in my insubstantial house,
your myth of hope,
the piece of man you left,
I live your death
stroke for stroke.

There are no vows you did not keep I will not break.
I leave no darkness unacknowledged for your sake.
You are the school I teach. The course I take.
I move toward age, and you become my son.
Along the path ahead
you lift aside
the branches.

WIDOW

You find in loss
all that you know you own for sure.
It is his absence where you are,
a scavenger among old days,
among the turned-up shoes,
the curving hands.

When will you throw away
the leavings, and let him be,
let him be through with you as he is finished
with his body,
and in the arctic of yourself
stand trusting, like the lilies?

HER ABSENCE

When she is gone and I'm in bed
my body turning without stop
against her body,

on lonely nights I roll around the world,
ease past myself on the other side at morning.

My eyes are helpless at their constant darting,
as if they had spun full round in their slick, curved walls,

and even the prodigal force of love
goes spuming along like a beachless sea,
breaking itself upon itself

till she return, and I return.

THE PEDAGOGICAL GUEST AND THE CHILD

"Take three round stones in your hand,
close your hand around the stones,
and at the mystic instant when
the congregation of your bones,
those doubting, drowsing, digital bones,
believe your stones are one round stone,
just one round stone with three round sides,
then you must open up again,
open your hand, open your hand
from *seem* to *be*, and count them:
three.
The fact abides."

"The fact abides.
But take my hand in your hand,
take my hand in your hand,
and when my hand
is a flutter of hands
and a flight of hands
and a sky of hands
close your hand."

MY DEAR, YOU'RE LIKE THIS PUBLIC PARK

The pigeons form a smart platoon
and waddle by in step and tune;
the courthouse clock has stopped at noon
and all is sweet obedience.
The dogs have learned some common sense,
there's no more howling through the fence:
they're not allowed to bite—why bark?

My dear, you're like this public park,
and we who wander through remark
how little's left that stirs or frightens.
Monumental water heightens
nicely out of nymphs and tritons
and the very shadows grow
with heads and shoulders in a row.

The bolted benches seem to know
their place. The pond's like safety glass.
The days like bright policemen pass,
and when at times a manic weed
starts crawling at heroic speed,
a jungle folded in its seed:
it smothers in the close-ranked grass.

PORTRAIT

All tactics, and no battlefields:
like the hiss when there's no gas to light the oven;
like a rich, unmarried man;
like living high
in Ada, Kansas.

RECOMMENDATIONS

This is a good fellow
   who knows what he may do?
He is most excited, he is walking
   the walls of himself
on tiptoe. Give him
   a prize.

And this one is steady;
   it is clear that he is breathing;
he will never kill any number
   of old ladies, nor harrow
hell. Give him
   a prize.

OTTERS

Out of water the polar bears loll their hot heads,
ducks creak, and I fidget. I'd like to be cool,
like to float with the ducks on the top of the stream;
dive and rise like a bear. But it's otters that bring
the most joy, and most absence of joy, which is horror.
They seem like my self out of love out of water.

And now they are drying it's no matter whether
they nuzzle or scurry or sleep. The zoo's sun
makes them stiff and ungainly, transforms the wet fur
to a substance as dull as the obverse of oil.

And we too are stranded, rough-surfaced and droll.
How we yearn for the feel of the smooth, naked plunge;
for the curve of pure meaning. Like otters we'd mean,
in a rush of the arc-spinning bones at the verge
of the pool, we'd sweep to a depth with their glide,
and flow with their flowing, act and its element one.

SUFFICIENT VISIT WITH THE SHOE CLERK'S BRIDE

We are visiting the shoe clerk's bride,
who wears her hair beehived, who smiles
like syrup spreading.

A shotgun visit in a room
with other humans, passing
words about like sweets.

And it is whispered how her clerk was led
to join *their* church to hear her singing
in the choir.

He now works late, her reconverted mate,
it is his after-Christmas sale;
but we must meet him, we must wait . . .

the talk goes stale,
like an old bread end that must be
thickly buttered: we are told

the number of stilettos he has sold,
and how he cries out in his sleep, how she awakes,
his hand upon her as he says:

"Pardon me, madam!
Would you like it with a medium
heel?"

And you so patient, smiling there,
and something in me saying
like a window up for air:

Why am I picked so proper? Why
have you taught me these
pauper's pieties?

Why have you made me all I fear?
What are we doing here?
Why did you bring me here?

KOREAN LORE

A queen it must have been,
disheartened by the strain of petty wars,
whose edict required an earthenware hat
with umbrella-sized brim
to be worn by all men.

Its weight would discourage a distant walk.
And as for talk, how close could one come
to a comrade? Surely her spies
would hear all conspiracies.

And if a hat were broken?
Decapitation!
So men stopped fighting
to care for their hats.

SONG OF THE LONG-MARRIED MAN

Son, said the long-married man,
a natural woman moves slow;
she sits and she tends to the clutch of the root
however the blossoms grow.

Get you a rare one, all speed,
and she'll run you like fire in dry grass.
But a good woman, give her a hand, help her up,
and the whole round world's stuck to her ass.

WHEN SHE IS DULL

When she is dull, my love, no force
can move her, she sits
upon the freeway like a load
of dung.

If troops of horse
clipped down upon her, if whole zoos
escaped . . . she'd sit,
an oxcart on its side, a cliff

at the turning. And yet
there is such beauty in her breath it catches mine.
I pause: declare my awe:
and she is gay.

WE BUILT A SHAKY HOUSE

We built a shaky house with no adorning
and said the house was large and gay and foursquare.
We took eyefuls of silence with our coffee:
oh, peace seemed handsome till we started learning
that walls of raucous roses whitewashed over
will bloom again, and love seek houses elsewhere.
We shut our eyes to find some room for turning.

We shut our eyes, and when we faced the morning
we found our only window double-lighted;
one casement granting each another vision
that called: *love, love!* Oh, then the house was burning.
We rushed through rooms that never seemed intended
for more than one, and both of us full-hearted.
We'd built a house that had no room for turning.

We'll build a better house; we'll take our warning
and let all angles intersect each other,
the walls adorned with many-colored roses.
Our new-made place will hold a world's sojourning,
and we the very members of the structure
will raise an honest roof against all weather
and dance while rooms dance with us, turning, turning.

THE GOLDEN AGE

I'll jest up a world, out of the two of us:
that my sperm spends
into you a billion
versions of me, racing
for home.

None smashes on the wall
of your slow, substantial egg,
but you bear them all,
and shortly
the world is looking very friendly.

You'd have a thousand sons an hour.
We'd run out of names!
Then there'd be daughters everywhere, as there are,
sitting to a meal,
basking on the beach all summer long.

A DREAM OF A GARDEN

for Sally Graham

1

At false dawn, when the moon whites the branches,
I walk the kindly garden of my dream,
and there community sustains me,
the poisons from my breath pass into leaves
that yield in turn my proper, altered air.

In such dependency and solitude the trees
prosper, and the tulips are cupped flame;
but we repine, we who became
the butchers of ourselves, though we were made
to pair, to dance, to clap, like hands, like feet.

Obscenities are chalked upon our walls.
They eat, eat through and bring foundations down.
This desert sea to sea, our brave home town,
was pulverized by lies; ill-coupled words
bred monsters; rabid dogs foamed from our speech.

Oh, we must tell ourselves a better story;
must chant the garden in the dream until it wakes.
For we have mucked-up daylight's garden, left
our beer cans condoms corpses tissue
everywhere.

The very scandals can't be spoken:
how old men masturbate their guns;
how young men pole
the vaginal hole
to return glued blind, poor wombward ones!

And a shallows the mind, a rock-shelf from horrors,
a nest of worms where were sharpened words
that promised to dig us
back to the sea.
All fever, all fever and fret the mind,

that once was a camel humped for the journey;
a store of riches; a honeyhead.

[68]

You know the void places where they sink,
those who despair of the possible city.
Pure brooding, hunched in on unhatchable self,
you know the cold trips of desperate men,
the girls thorned at angles off from the source.

They plunge to be lonely: from stink of words
would not take infection; would sell no praise
nailed in a room with a painted smile
on the door. They'd kill, they'd kill to be real.
The milk curds like cancer, dammed in the breast.

And I who would sing out a vision, I hear
a thump between spaces, brute fist of heart,
and say we must love, as if to a fish
full landed I'd preach, keening *Smoothed-down bird,*
sleek into speed as your element,

speed into love, and if by sand
burned raw at first, so earn the sea,
swimming sand; your flesh is free
to move, to move through what moist it can get
from inside out, in the salt of its sweat.

Advise all to love: like Dante's light
in hell, convention untrue to condition;
so distant the source, so sunk the ocean;
God hums such songs in the wintertime
when the journal reads nothing, nothing to keep.

Mirage of a garden. Who'd waste his spit
on this? The children turn toward Nod,
where Nod blazes tawny, tranced in its dust;
where the sting of the pores is bathed in sleep,
and the strength-crazed root is fed by blood.

Where we walk, we must drag our rivers behind us;
meeting together; a pool of streams.

3

We toss in such questions as in a bed
ordained for sweetness, landlords of seeds
in slim beds dreaming a birth come back,
dreaming again a possible city
with fearless birds and hosts of friends.

What seeks to sing, that put we hope in;
what seeks to sing and would not cease.
What urges concord, the raising of walls
like the skins of God: that hammers build,
that sheaves be passed from hand to hand.

A dream of a garden. Whatever proceeds
to make these offers, *that* put we hope in;
what gives us pause at mere survival,
mere numbering of goods and days,
of goods and days baled up like straw;

what seeks to sing
and would not cease.

OCTOBER

My wife sits reading in a garden chair
Pope's *Moral Essays* by the failing light,
as leaves turn epileptic in the air
and through the woods come poachers, and the night.

Pope's natural habitat: a bullet rips
the homespun silence and the volume slips,
but catching it she finds her place in time
and never drops the stitches of a rhyme.

Braving the season for the sake of wit,
she holds each couplet in such close esteem
no maniac can put a hole in it.
The year's in tatters, but she makes a seam;

the house is civil, though the wood's insane,
and man's the missing link who lets the chain-
of-being shake. It's hanging by a hair.
My wife sits reading in a garden chair.